MW00572740

Tweed suits soft as the Afghan's coat

January 1956

Vintage VOGUE: 24 postcards to color in Illustration by Iain R. Webb
Published by Conran Octopus Ltd © The Condé Nast Publications Ltd 2016

Floating silk for a
delicious party dress

May 1954

Vintage VOGUE: 24 postcards to color in Illustration by Iain R. Webb
Published by Conran Octopus Ltd © The Condé Nast Publications Ltd 2016

Great allure in a short evening dress

March 1950

Vintage VOGUE: 24 postcards to color in Illustration by Iain R. Webb
Published by Conran Octopus Ltd © The Condé Nast Publications Ltd 2016

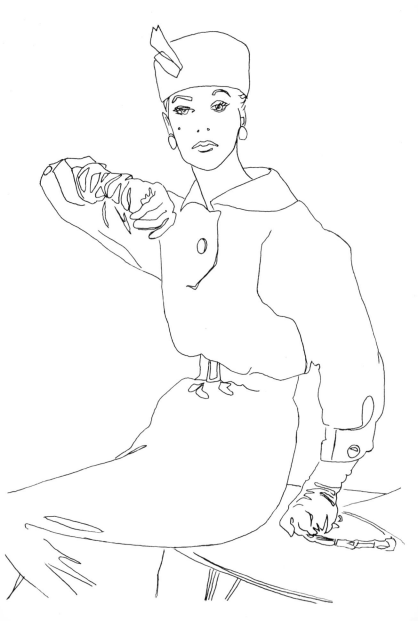

The blouson dress is the freshest silhouette

August 1958

Vintage VOGUE: 24 postcards to color in Illustration by Iain R. Webb
Published by Conran Octopus Ltd © The Condé Nast Publications Ltd 2016

An enchanting mob-cap:
very young, very pretty

March 1958

Vintage VOGUE: 24 postcards to color in Illustration by Iain R. Webb

Published by Conran Octopus Ltd © The Condé Nast Publications Ltd 2016

The English suit
is slim but easy

September 1951

Penguin sleeves make
a striking feature

November 1951

Vintage VOGUE: 24 postcards to color in Illustration by Iain R. Webb
Published by Conran Octopus Ltd © The Condé Nast Publications Ltd 2016

Geranium red adds
Christmas color

December 1957

Vintage VOGUE: 24 postcards to color in Illustration by Iain R. Webb
Published by Conran Octopus Ltd © The Condé Nast Publications Ltd 2016

This season's newest and gayest coat

February 1959

Vintage VOGUE: 24 postcards to color in Illustration by Iain R. Webb
Published by Conran Octopus Ltd © The Condé Nast Publications Ltd 2016

A black dress and jacket are winter mainstays

November 1957

Vintage VOGUE: 24 postcards to color in Illustration by Iain R. Webb
Published by Conran Octopus Ltd © The Condé Nast Publications Ltd 2016

Team an all-day dress with plain accessories

September 1950

Vintage VOGUE: 24 postcards to color in Illustration by Iain R. Webb
Published by Conran Octopus Ltd © The Condé Nast Publications Ltd 2016

Pearls and parma violets are frankly feminine

January 1952

Vintage VOGUE: 24 postcards to color in Illustration by Iain R. Webb
Published by Conran Octopus Ltd © The Condé Nast Publications Ltd 2016

Fill a wide neckline with a chiffon blouse

March 1957

Vintage VOGUE: 24 postcards to color in Illustration by Iain R. Webb
Published by Conran Octopus Ltd © The Condé Nast Publications Ltd 2016

Metallic silk for an Oriental slant

March 1957

Vintage VOGUE: 24 postcards to color in Illustration by Iain R. Webb
Published by Conran Octopus Ltd © The Condé Nast Publications Ltd 2016

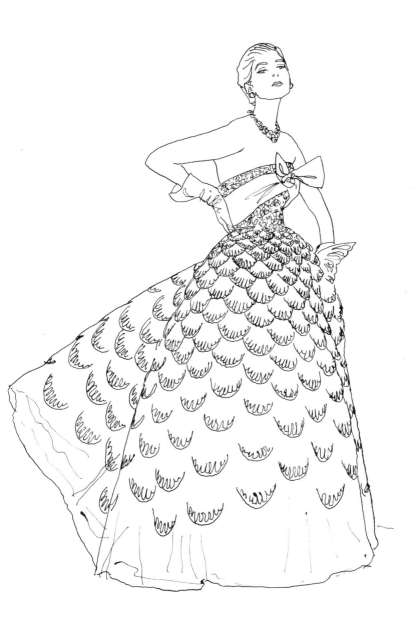

For drama add a bow
across the bodice

October 1951

Vintage VOGUE: 24 postcards to color in Illustration by Iain R. Webb
Published by Conran Octopus Ltd © The Condé Nast Publications Ltd 2016

Elegance sums up
the season

September 1954

Vintage VOGUE: 24 postcards to color in Illustration by Iain R. Webb
Published by Conran Octopus Ltd © The Condé Nast Publications Ltd 2016

The latest line is flat bosomed and demure

September 1954

Vintage VOGUE: 24 postcards to color in Illustration by Iain R. Webb
Published by Conran Octopus Ltd © The Condé Nast Publications Ltd 2016

The biggest bow
in the world

December 1951

Vintage VOGUE: 24 postcards to color in Illustration by Iain R. Webb
Published by Conran Octopus Ltd © The Condé Nast Publications Ltd 2016

Adaptability relies on pitch-perfect accessories

April 1959

Vintage VOGUE: 24 postcards to color in Illustration by Iain R. Webb
Published by Conran Octopus Ltd © The Condé Nast Publications Ltd 2016

Casual chic demands
scene-stealing jewels

October 1955

Vintage VOGUE: 24 postcards to color in Illustration by Iain R. Webb
Published by Conran Octopus Ltd © The Condé Nast Publications Ltd 2016

The prettiest summer
for years

June 1954

Vintage VOGUE: 24 postcards to color in Illustration by Iain R. Webb
Published by Conran Octopus Ltd © The Condé Nast Publications Ltd 2016

Stripes step out
on the town

July 1954

Vintage VOGUE: 24 postcards to color in Illustration by Iain R. Webb
Published by Conran Octopus Ltd © The Condé Nast Publications Ltd 2016

A trapeze suit
depends on cut

August 1958

Vintage VOGUE: 24 postcards to color in Illustration by Iain R. Webb
Published by Conran Octopus Ltd © The Condé Nast Publications Ltd 2016